Colour to Life...

Pirkei Avos:

Ethics of our Fathers

Chapter 1

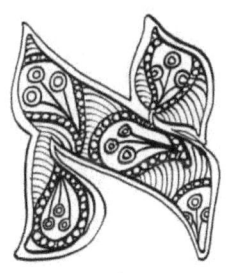

ISBN-10: 1519286171
ISBN-13: 978-1519286178

goldabrenner@gmail.com

Compiled and illustrated by Golda Brenner

Translations of Pirkei Avos belong to – and are
being used with permission from The
Meaningful Life Centre
www.meaningfullife.com

Introduction

Adult colouring in books have exploded with popularity. It's the new trend in 'creative meditations' or 'art therapy'. Why are they so popular? For some it is a stress relief and for others, it brings one back to an enjoyable and familiar childhood activity, which has now become socially acceptable for adults to do also.

I was introduced to adult colouring books by my Mother who came out of a bookstore one day and gave me a little book which was full of pictures. On one side was a quote from a celebrity or poet, and on the corresponding page was a pattern or picture. The idea was that you meditate on the quote while colouring in. I started using the book and found that I really enjoyed clearing my mind and simply colouring in. The concentration and focus which is applied is a grounding process and a mindful exercise.

My studies and many years of experience working with children and more recently with the Montessori approach have revealed a strong appreciation for activities which are process valued rather than outcome valued. I believe that this type of exercise is a healthy way to calm the mind and would be particularly useful for those who suffer from short term concentration or stress.

As I worked slowly through my colouring book, I wondered how much more effective and relevant this exercise would be to me, if I was meditating on Jewish quotes. I did a little research and found no Jewish adult colour in books hence I started this project 'Colour to life..'

The Lubavitcher Rebbe often emphasized the importance of learning Pirket Avos – "Ethics of our Fathers" and as a part of the Jewish people, I feel so blessed to have an original and universal guide on morals and ethics to refer to.

This project became a creative outlet, an opportunity for Torah study and I have enjoyed the entire process! I hope that you can find your own value in this book and utilize it simply as a foundation to express your own emotions, creativity and mindful exploration!

How to

Take a few deep breaths and try to clear your mind before you start. Turn your phone off and allocate yourself some time for this exercise –build up to 10 min of pure concentration each day.

Each quote corresponds to a picture.

Read the quote and try to meditate on it while you colour in. You will find that your mind will wander and that's ok, just try and keep going back to the quote.

Something you can think about to keep focused, is how the picture relates to the words, your own interpretation on the relationship between the words and the picture.

Take your time colouring, practice care and be deliberate.
Remember: it's all about the process – not the outcome!

There is plenty of space for you to practice and explore your own creativity through drawing or writing.

To protect the pages that follow, use a piece of cardboard (you can cut from an old shoebox) behind the page you are colouring at the time.

I also suggest that you invest in good quality colouring pencils to enhance your experience.

Acknowledgements

Thank you to my mother who has taught me appreciation.

My journey towards appreciating my heritage is greatly enhanced and inspired by the writings of the Lubavitcher Rebbe.

Ultimate gratitude to our creator who blesses us with the ability to create.

Moses received the Torah from Sinai and gave it over to Joshua. Joshua gave it over to the Elders, the Elders to the Prophets, and the Prophets gave it over to the Men of the Great Assembly. They [the Men of the Great Assembly] would always say these three things:

Be cautious in judgment.
Establish many pupils.
And make a safety fence around the Torah.

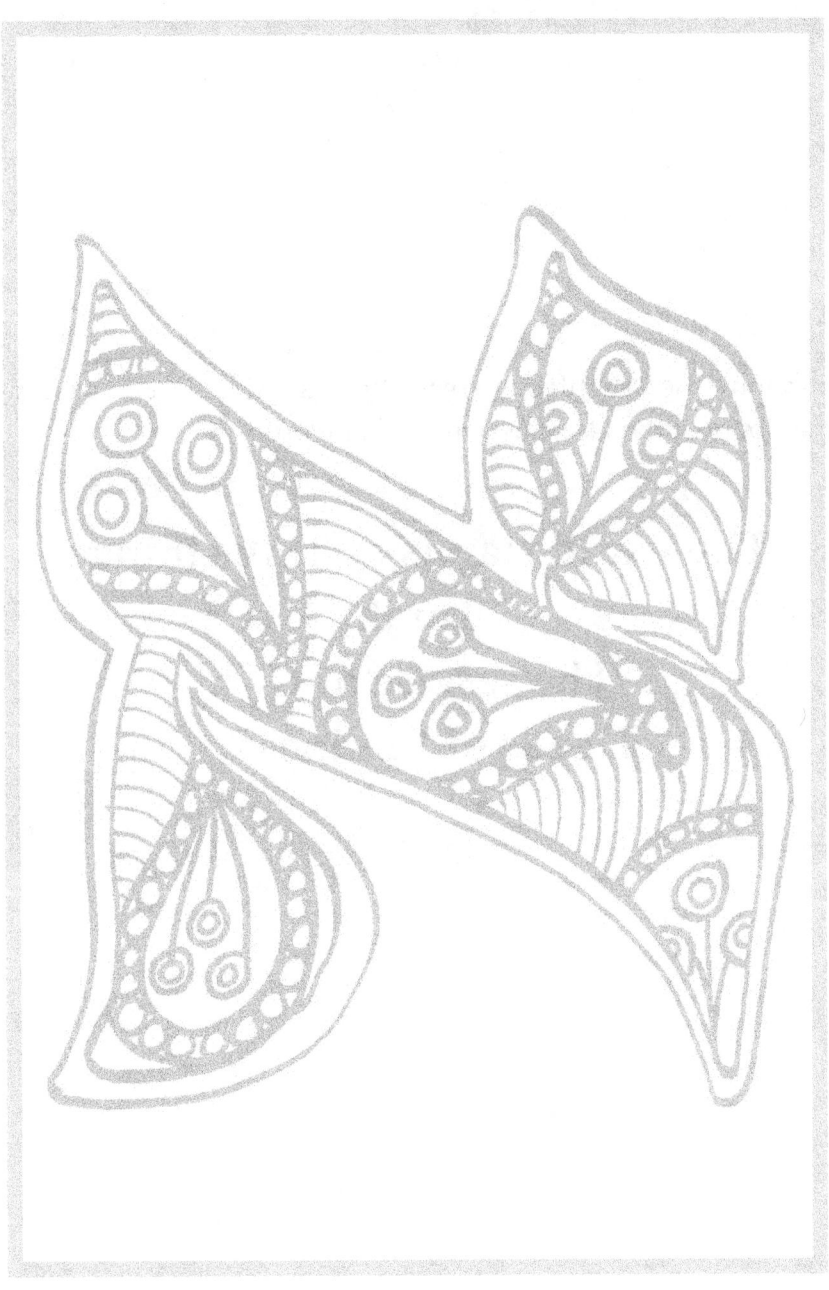

Shimon the Righteous was among the last surviving members of the Great assembly. He would say:

The world stands on three things:
Torah,
The service of G-d,
Deeds of kindness.

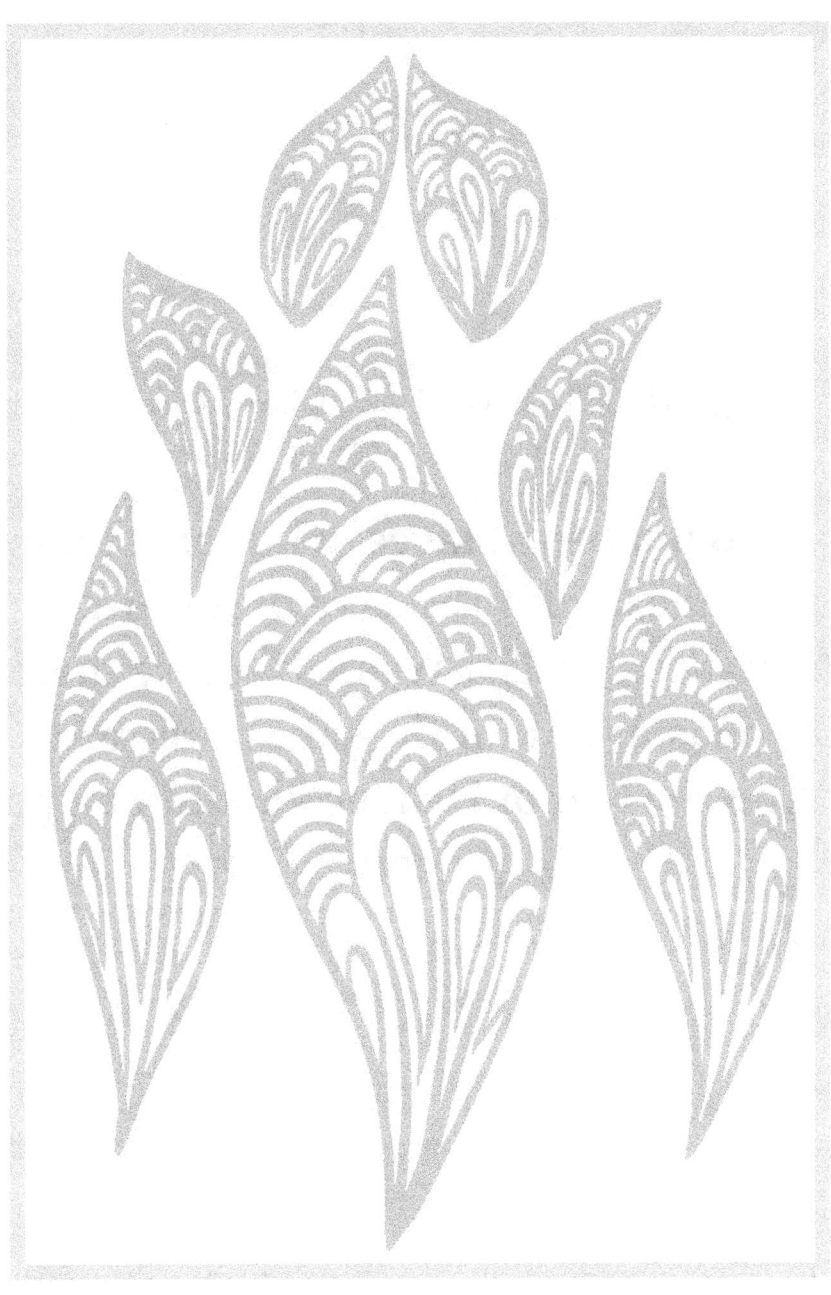

Antignos of Socho received the tradition from Shimon the Righteous. He would say:

Do not be as slaves, who serve their master for the sake of reward. Rather, be as slaves who serve their master not for the sake of reward. And the fear of Heaven should be upon you.

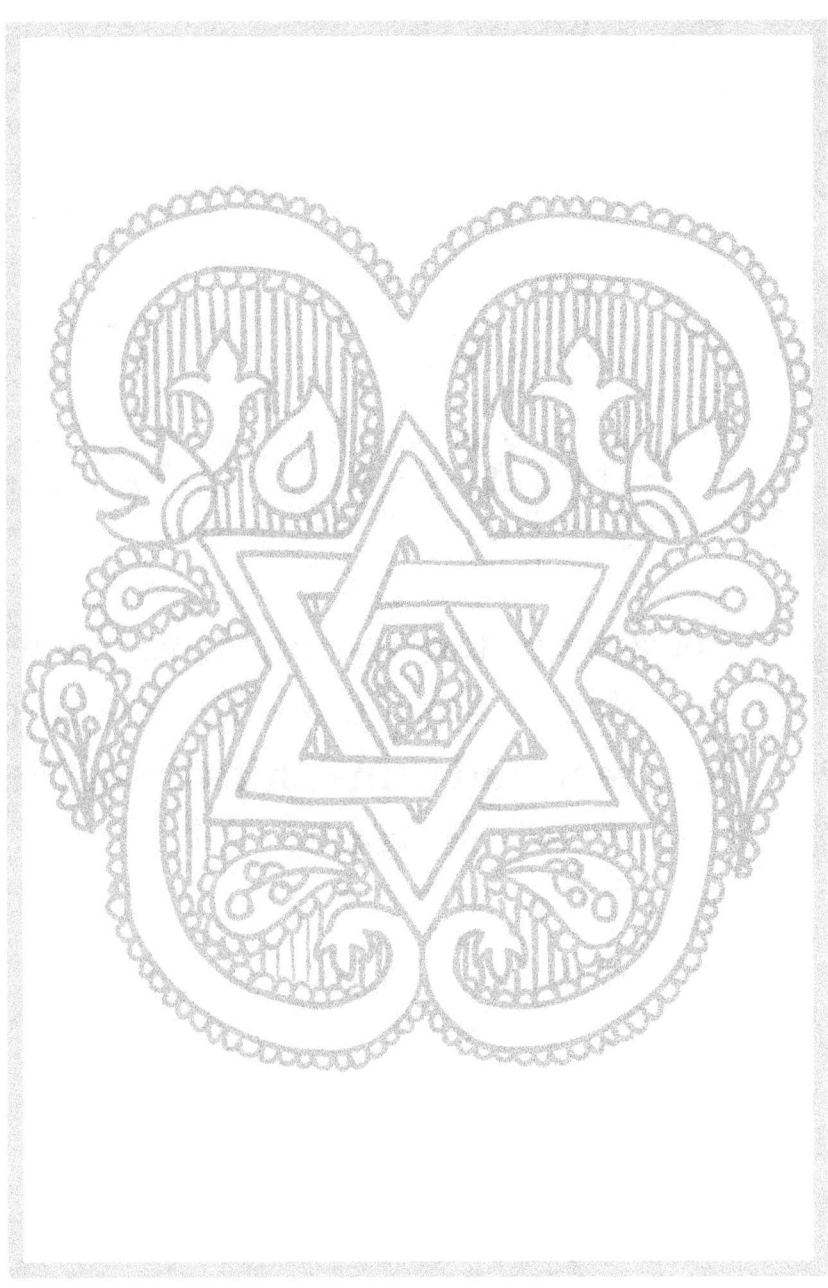

Yossei the son of Yoezer of Tzreidah, and Yossei the son of Yochanan of Jerusalem, received the tradition from them. Yossei the son of Yoezer of Tzreidah would say:

Let your home be a meeting place for the wise; dust yourself in the soil of their feet, and drink thirstily of their words.

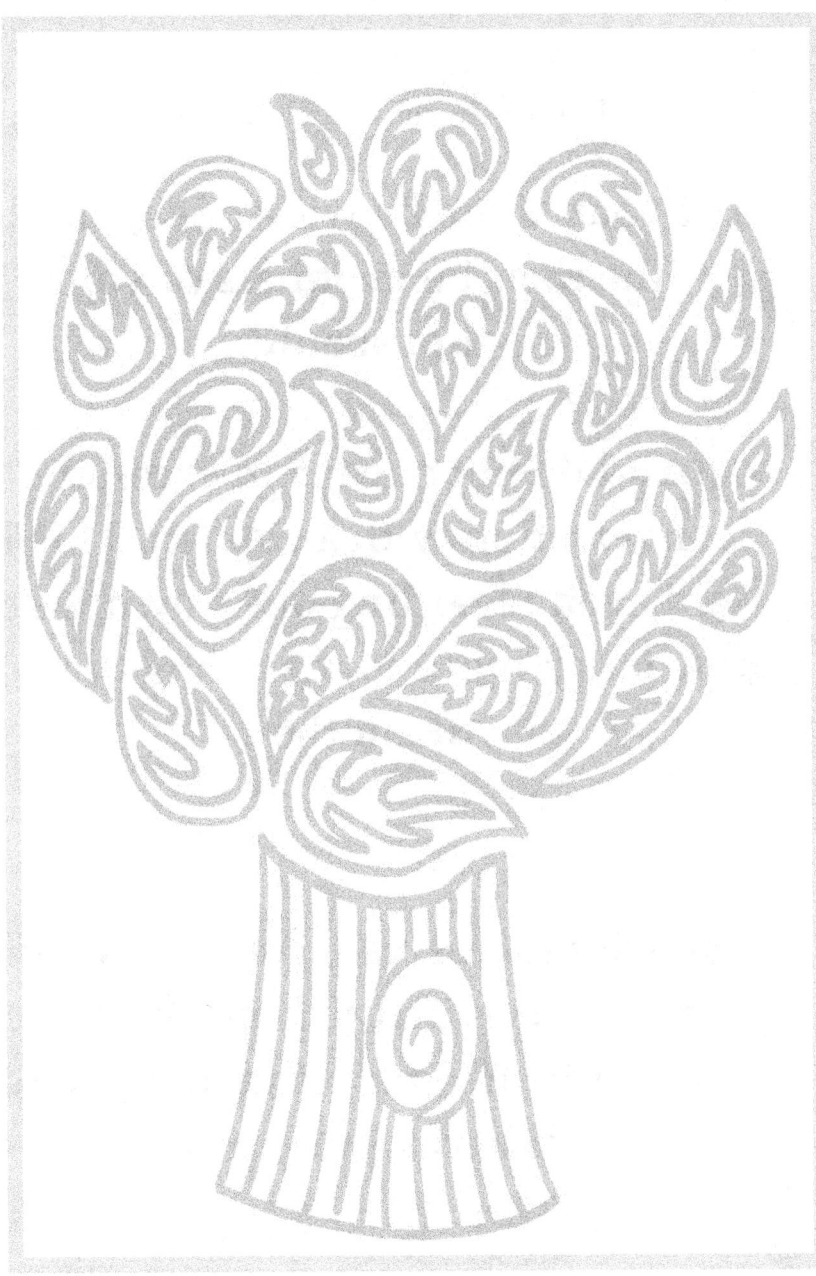

Yossei the son of Yochanan of Jerusalem would say:

Let your home be wide open, and let the poor be members of your household.

And do not engage in excessive conversation with a woman. This is said even regarding one's own wife-- how much more so regarding the wife of another.

Hence, the sages said:

One who excessively converses with a woman causes evil to himself, neglects the study of Torah, and, in the end, inherits purgatory.

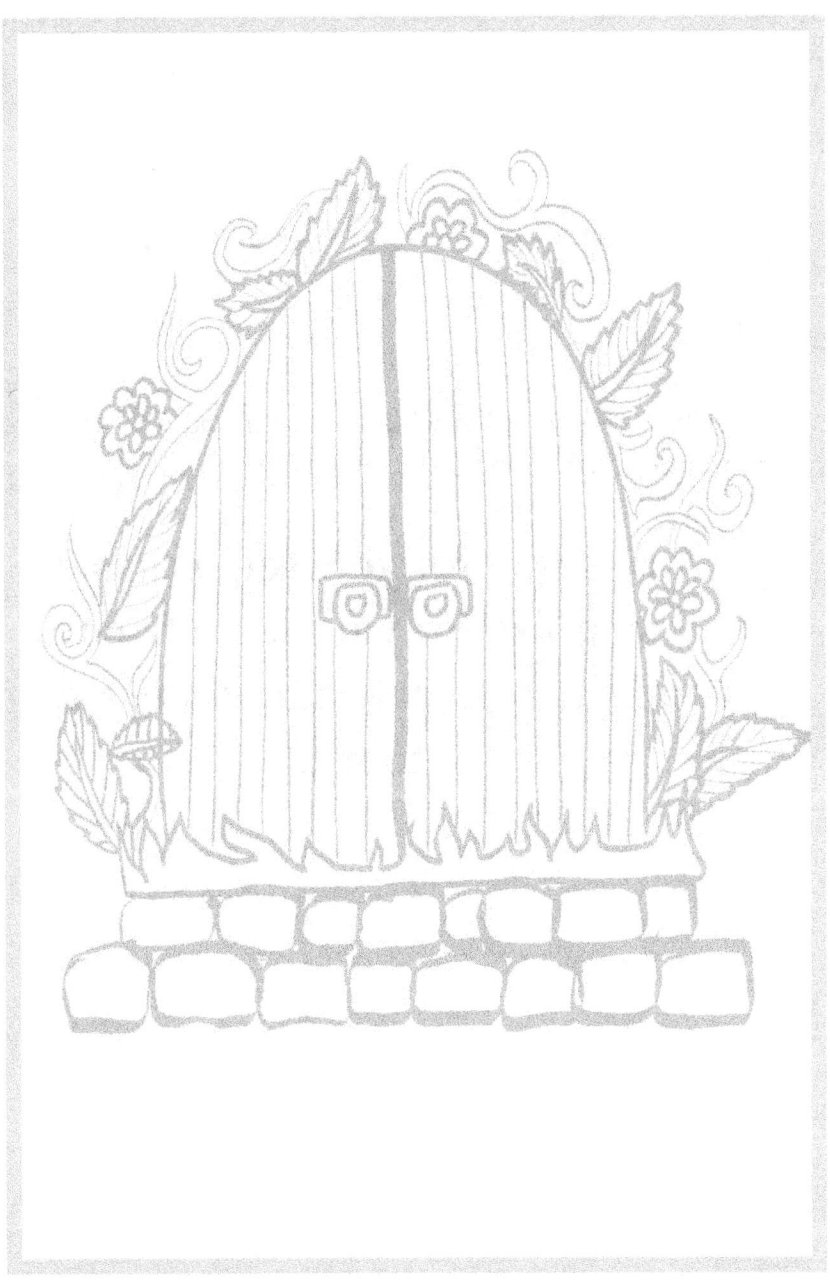

Joshua the son of Perachia and Nitai the Arbelite received from them. Joshua the son of Perachia would say:

Assume for yourself a master, acquire for yourself a friend, and judge every man to the side of merit.

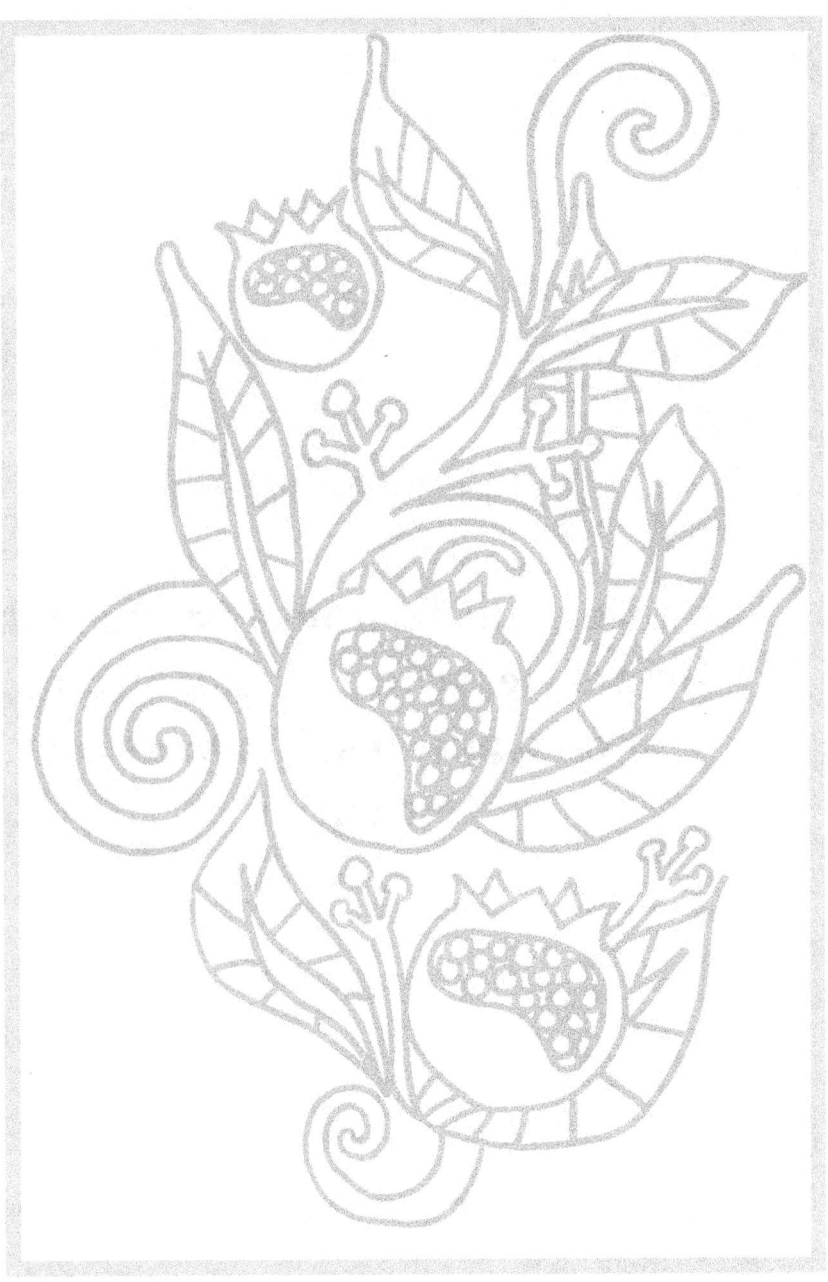

Nitai the Arbelite would say:

Distance yourself from a bad neighbor, do not cleave to a wicked person, and do not abandon belief in retribution.

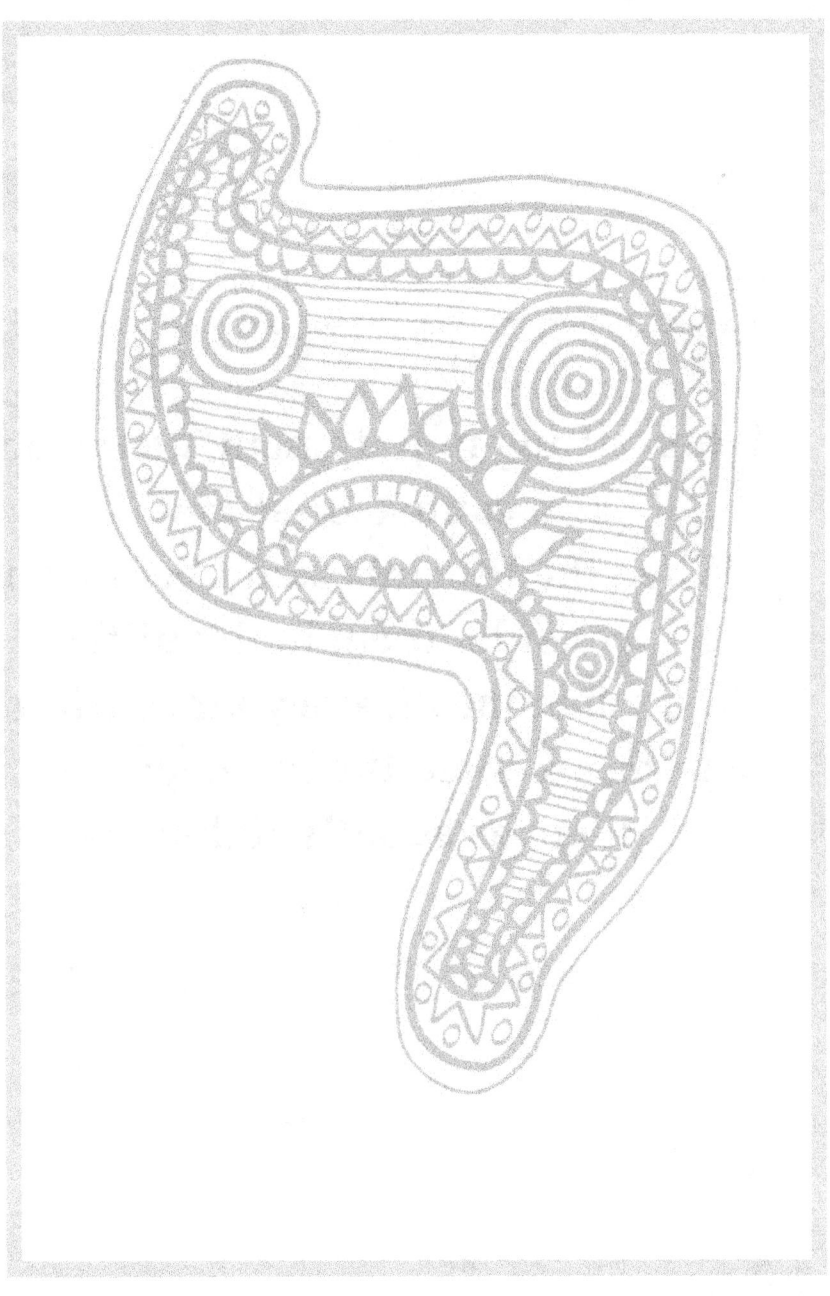

Judah the son of Tabbai and Shimon the son of Shotach received from them. Judah the son of Tabbai would say:

When sitting in judgment, do not act as a counselor-at-law.
When the litigants stand before you, consider them both guilty;
And when they leave your courtroom, having accepted the judgment, regard them as equally righteous.

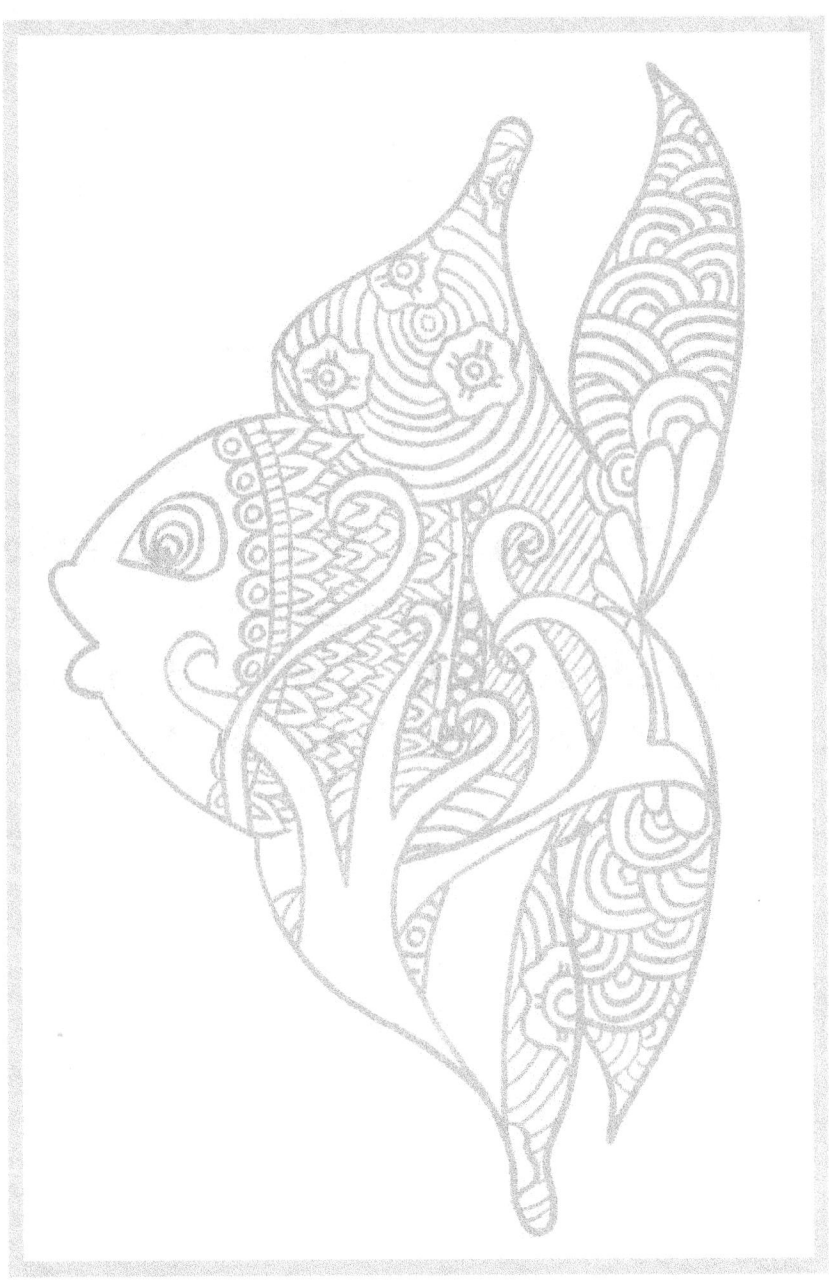

Shimon the son of Shotach would say:

**Increasingly cross-examine the witnesses.
Be careful with your words, lest they
learn from them how to lie.**

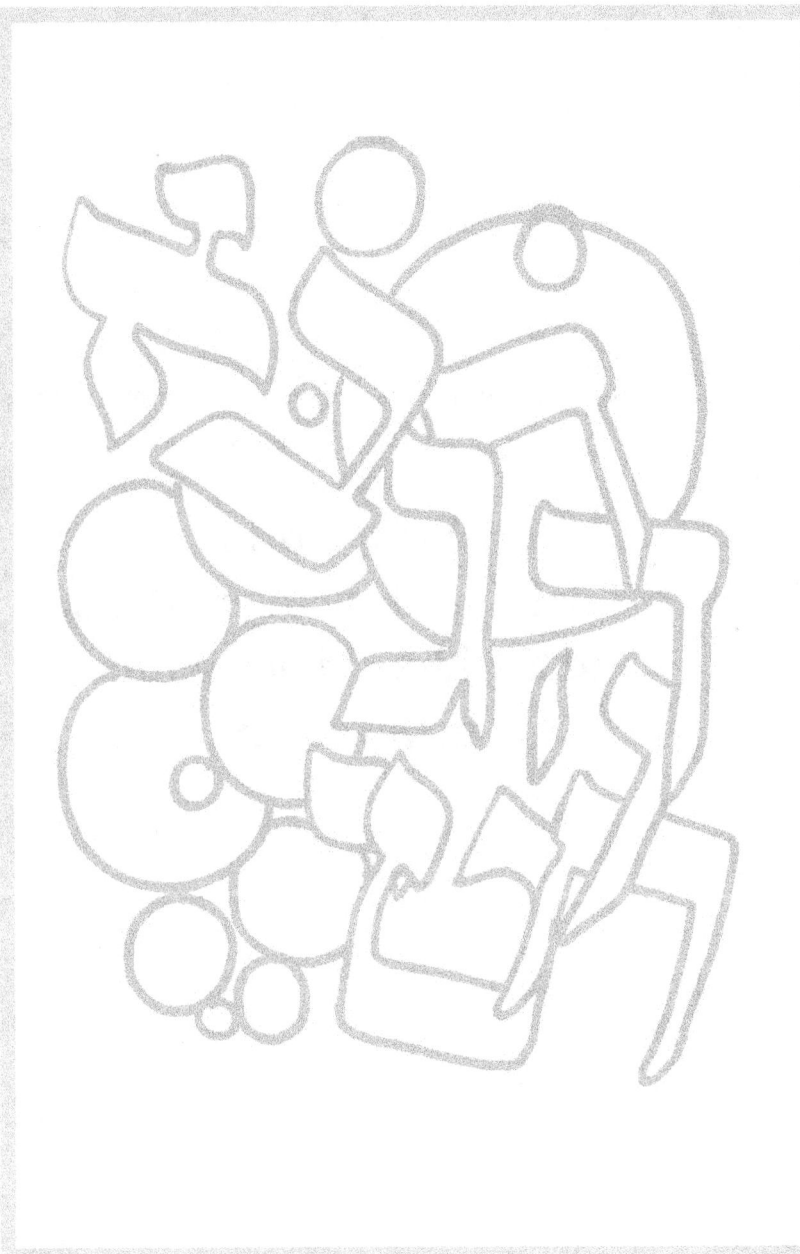

Shmaayah and Avtalyon received from them.
Shmaayah would say:

Love work,
Loath mastery over others,
and avoid intimacy with the
government.

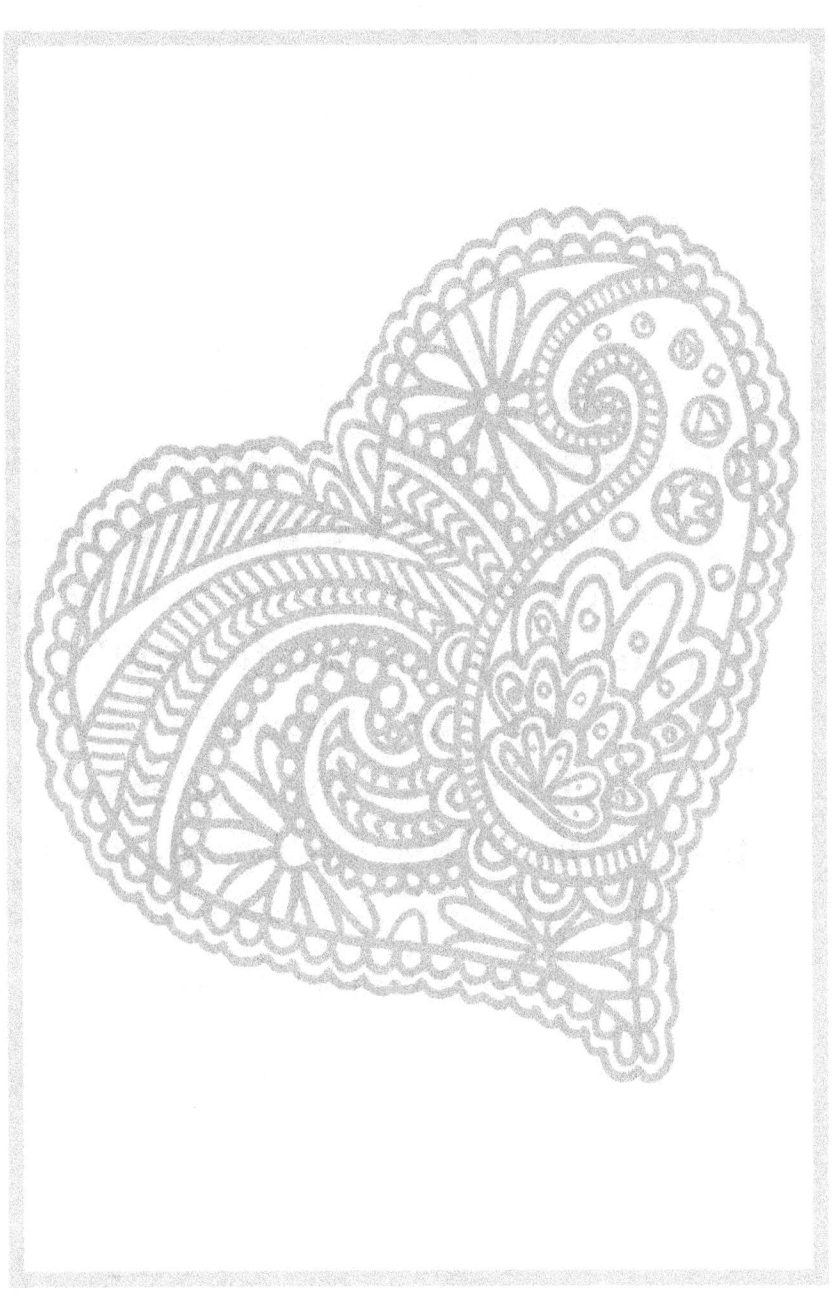

Avtalyon would say:

Scholars, be careful with your words. For you may be exiled to a place inhabited by evil elements [who will distort your words to suit their negative purposes]. The disciples who come after you will then drink of these evil waters and be destroyed, and the Name of Heaven will be desecrated.

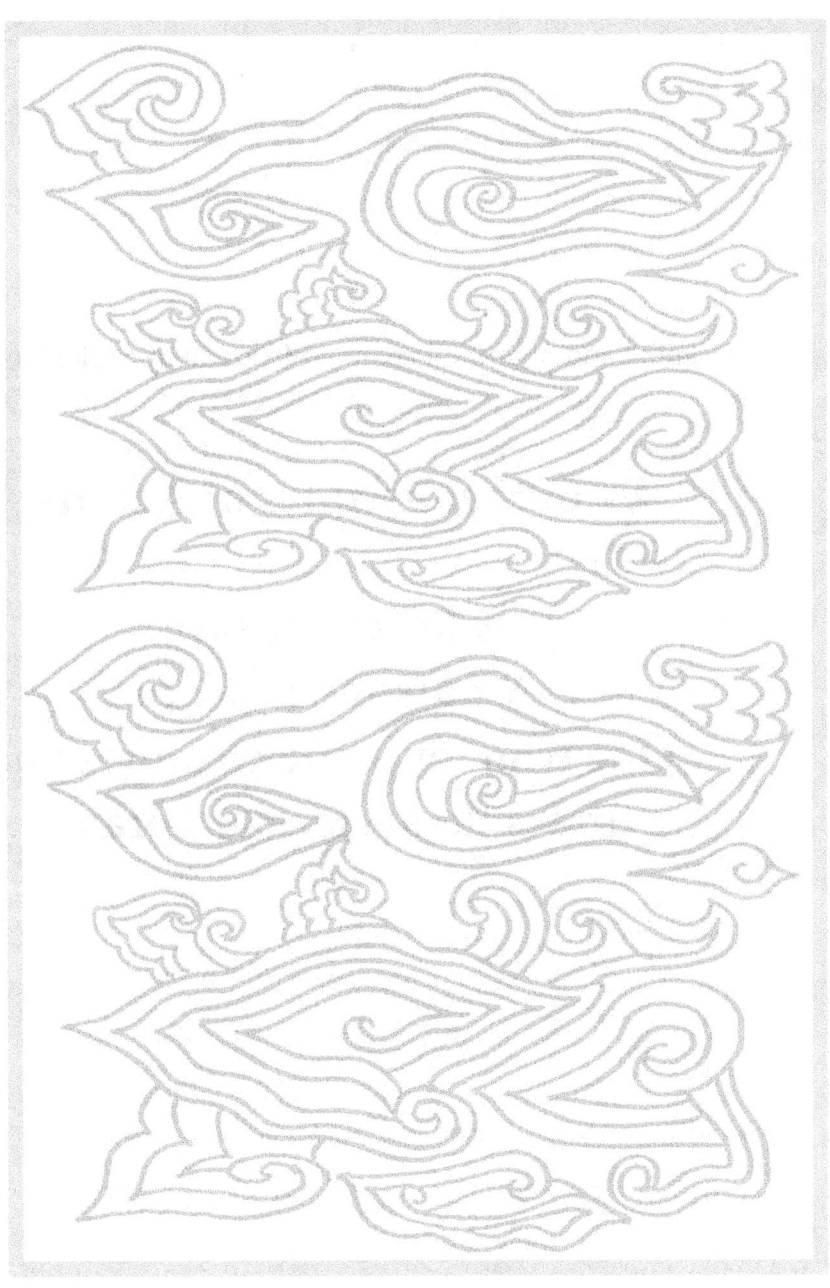

Hillel and Shammai received from them. Hillel would say:

Be of the disciples of Aaron—

A lover of peace,
A pursuer of peace,
One who loves the creatures and draws them close to Torah.

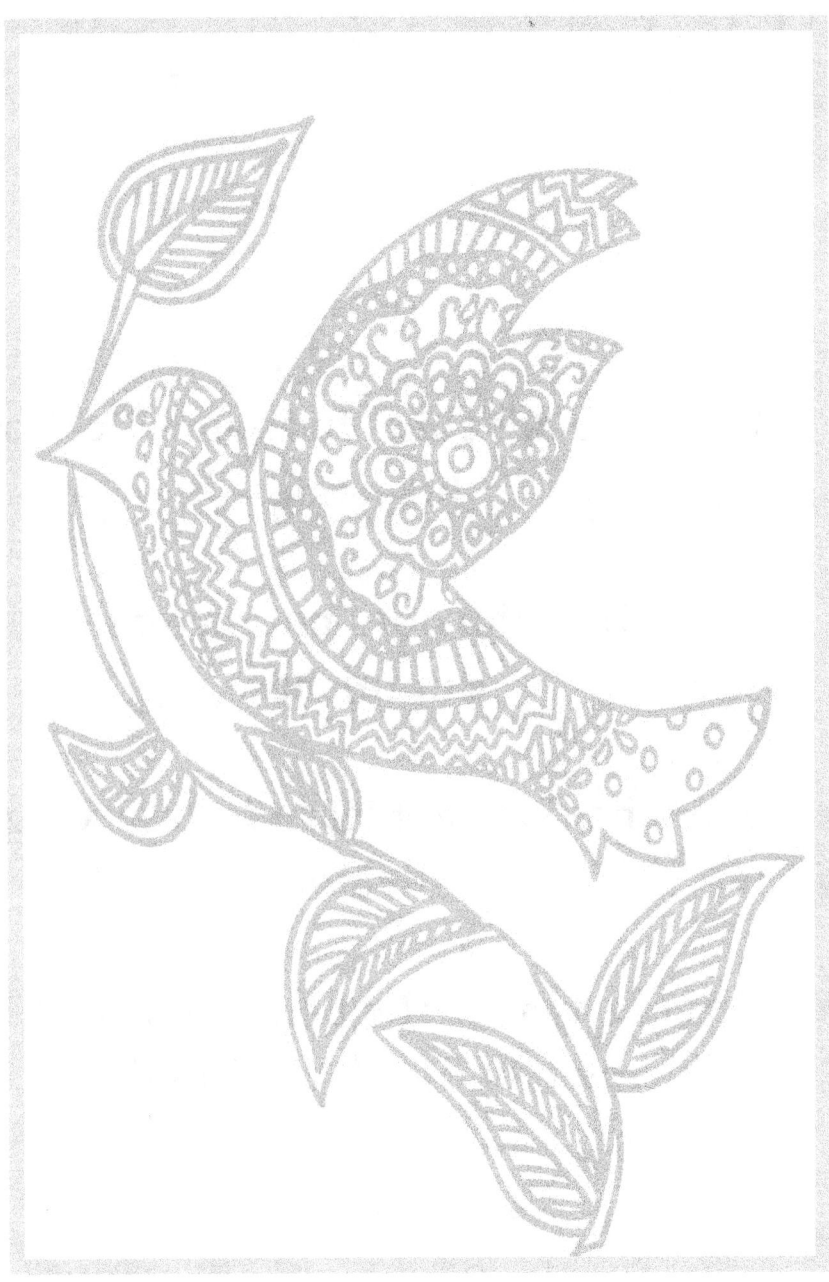

He would also say:

One who advances his name, destroys his name.

One who does not increase, diminishes.

One who does not learn is deserving of death.

And one who make personal use of the crown of Torah shall perish.

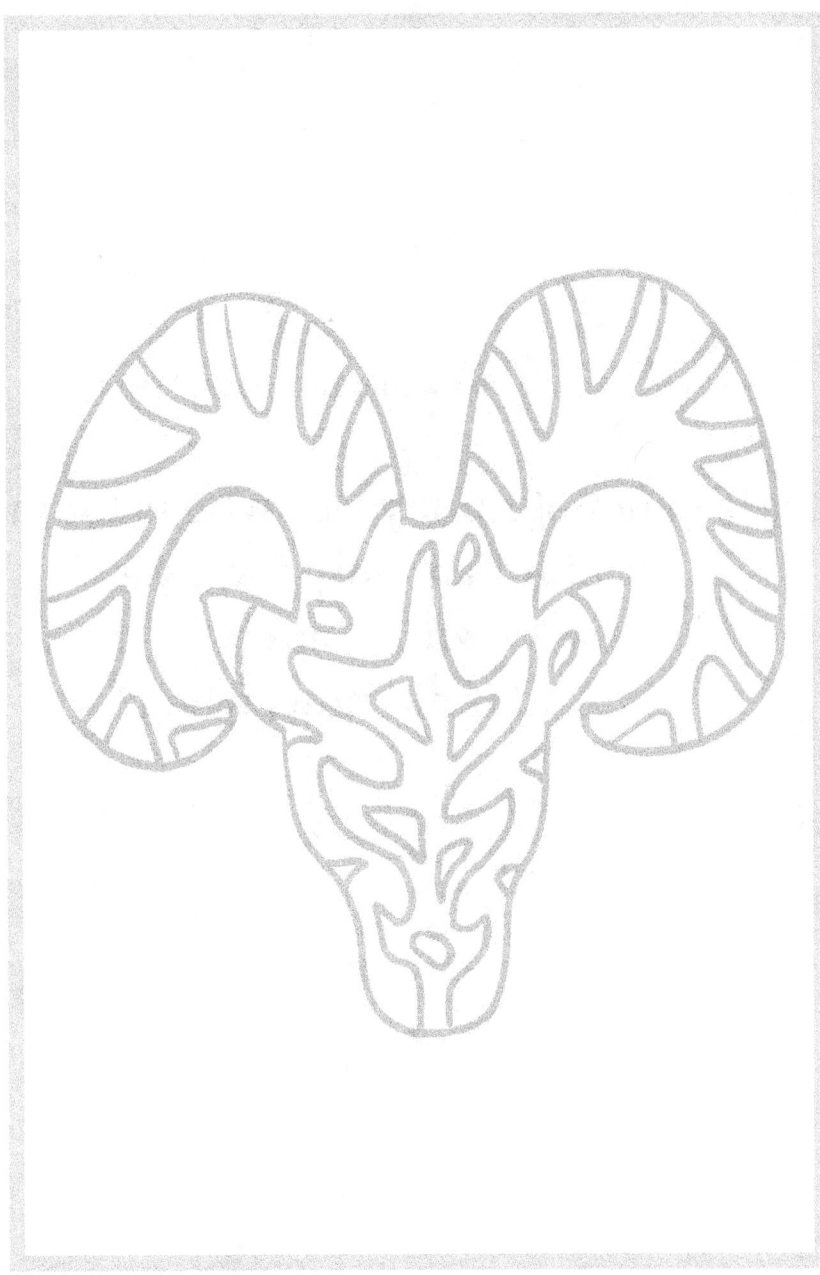

He would also say:

If I am not for myself, who is for me?
And if I am only for myself,
what am I?
And if not now, when?

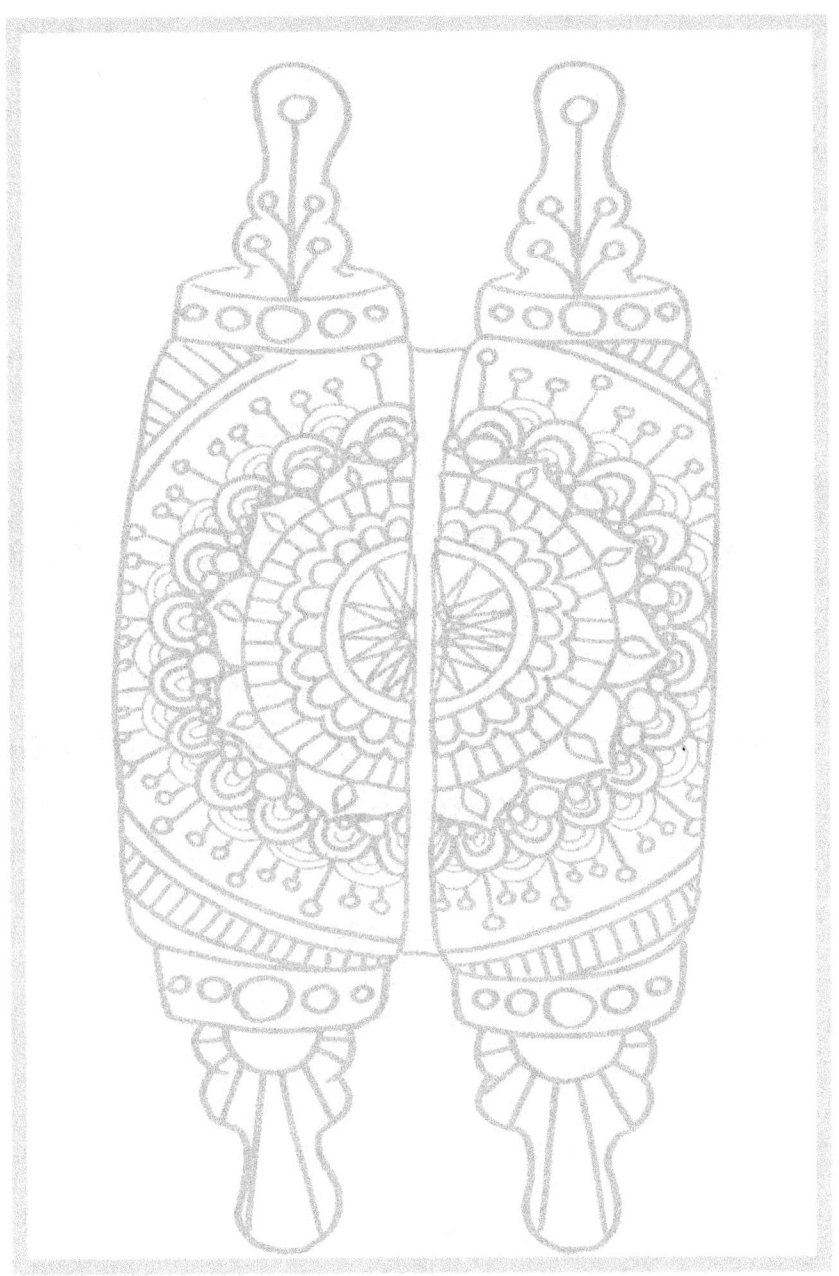

Shammai would say:

**Make your torah study a permanent
fixture of your life.
Say little and do much.
And receive every man with a pleasant
countenance.**

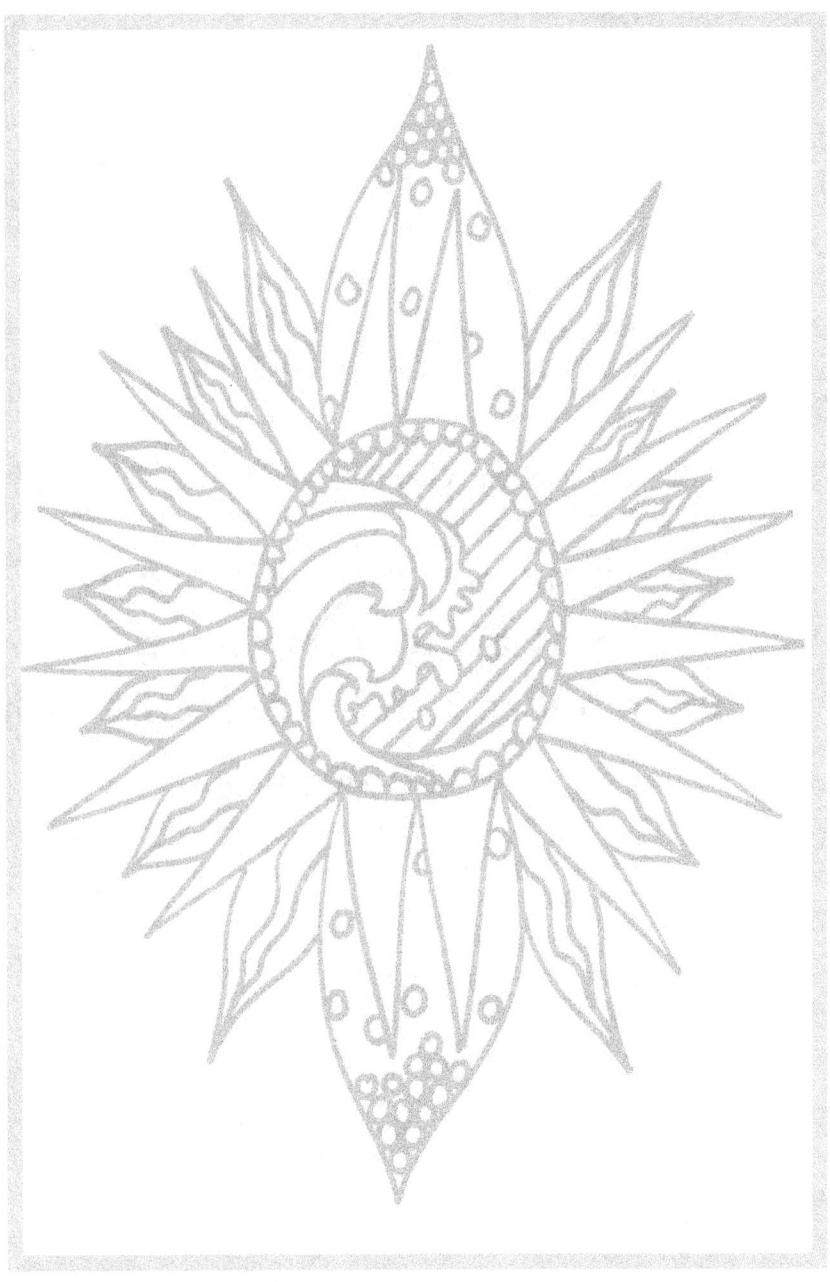

Rabban Gamliel would say:

Assume for yourself a master;
Stay away from doubt;
And do not accustom yourself to tithe
by estimation.

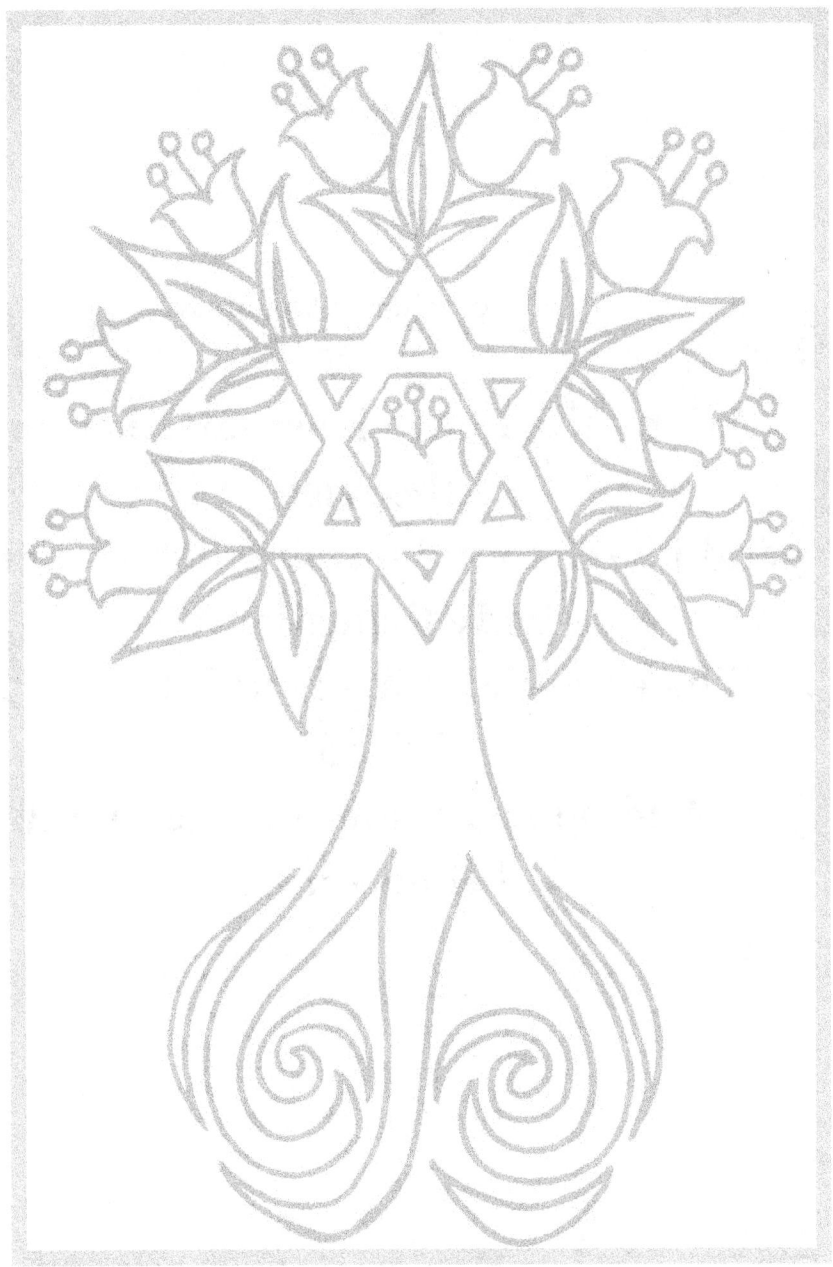

His son, Shimon, would say:

All my life I have been raised among the wise, and I have found nothing better for the body than silence. The essential thing is not study, but deed. And one who speaks excessively brings on sin.

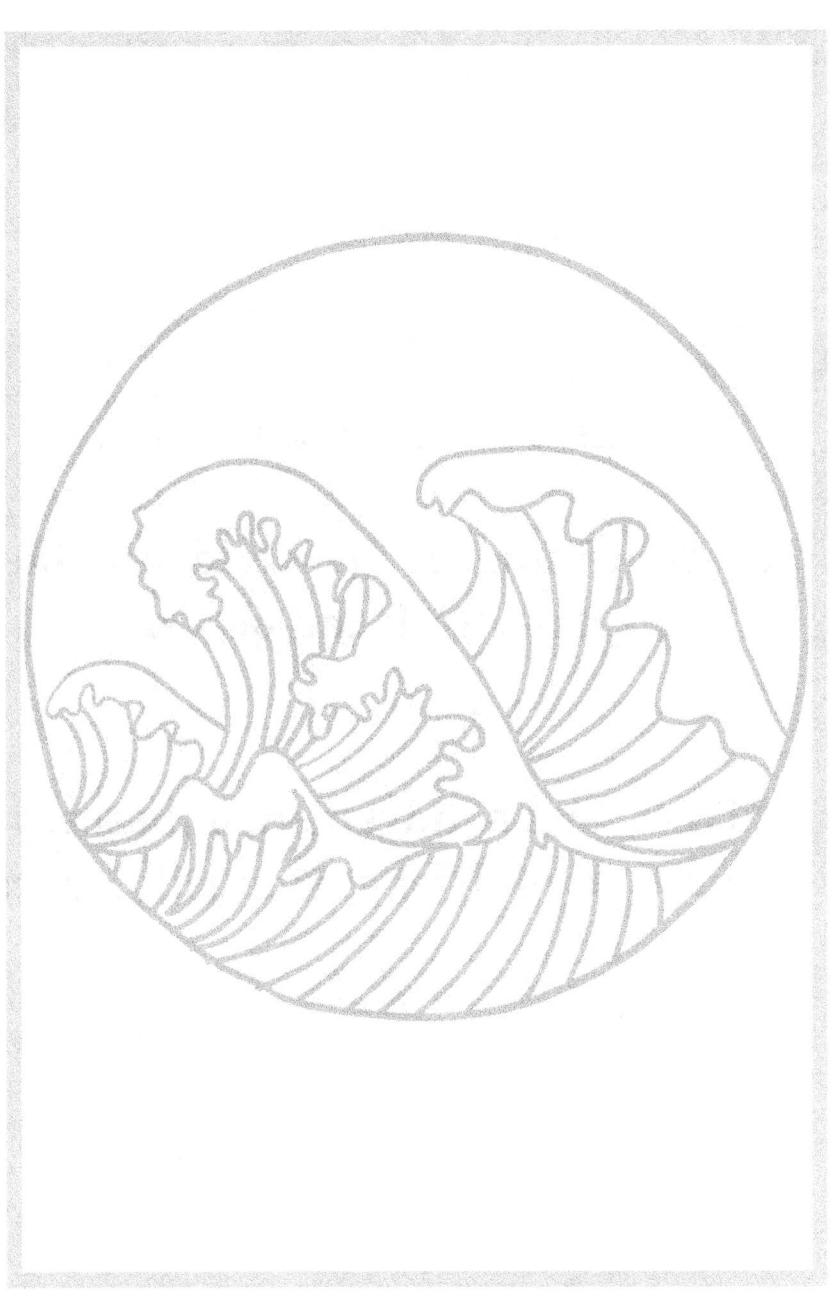

Rabbi Shimon the son of Gamliel would say:

By three things is the world sustained: law, truth and peace.

As is stated (Zachariah 8:16):

"Truth, and a judgement of peace, you should administer at your [city] gates."

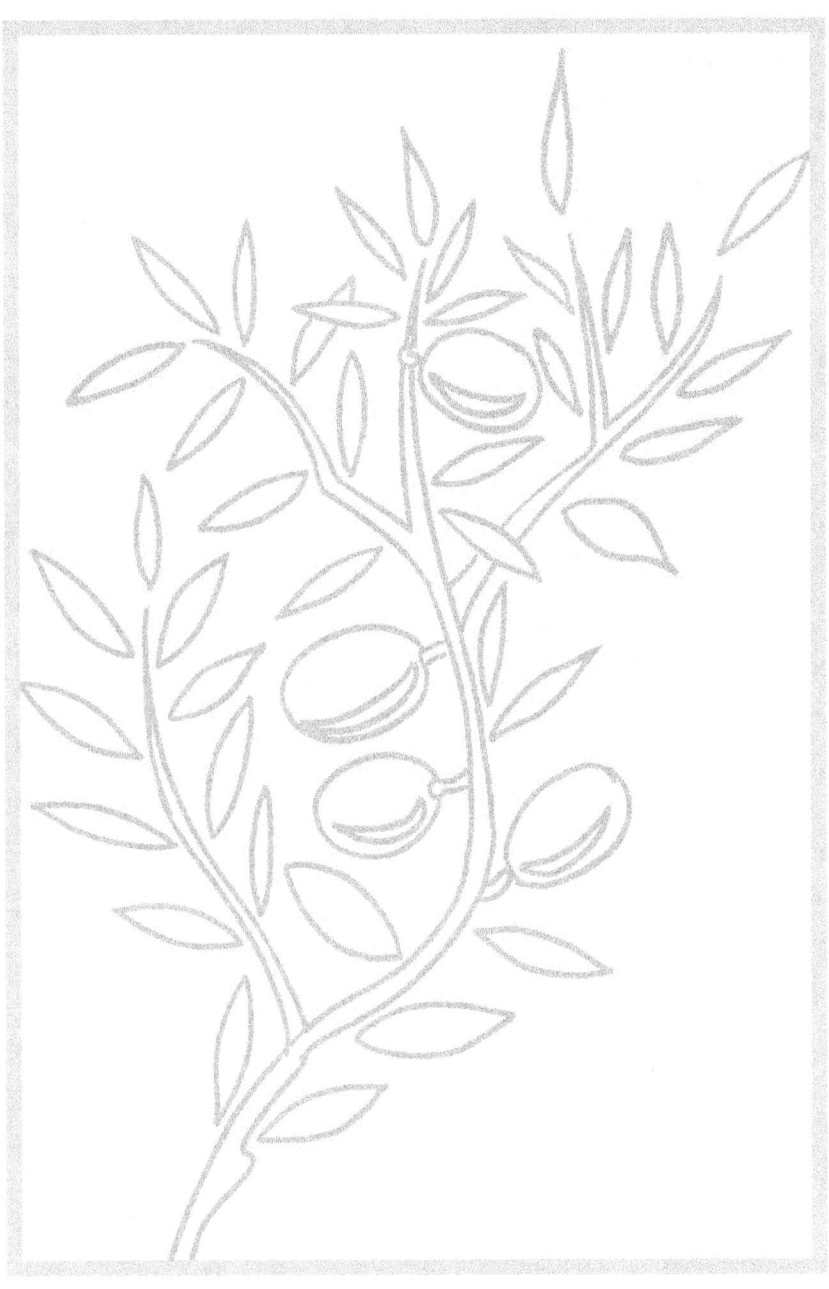

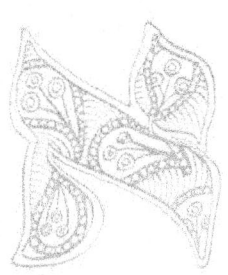

www.ingramcontent.com/pod-product-compliance
Lightning Source LLC
Chambersburg PA
CBHW051225170526
45166CB00005B/2041